CARTOONS FROM PLAYBOY

GOOD-BYE, CRUEL WORLD

by

Howard Shoemaker

PAN BOOKS LTD : LONDON

First published 1971 simultaneously in the United States of America and Canada by Playboy Press, Chicago, Illinois.

This edition published 1972 by Pan Books Ltd, 33 Tothill Street, London, SW1.

ISBN 0 330 23225 8

Printed in Great Britain
by Fletcher & Son Ltd, Norwich

PREFACE

Howard Shoemaker's first cartoon sale was to PLAYBOY; it appeared in the magazine's August 1960 issue. Prior to that event, he had been strictly a commercial artist and graphic designer. He considers it a major turning-point in his life, for 'cartooning is the only thing I've ever done that I haven't had to sell out in'.

He was born in Council Bluffs, Iowa, and for many years has lived just across the river in Omaha, Nebraska. He received no formal education past the high-school level and no art training. His early work, he says, 'looked as if it were drawn with a wet cigar', and so he set about teaching himself the rudiments of anatomy, since he is a firm believer in the axiom that one must know the rules before one may break them.

A jazz saxophonist of professional calibre, he was once tempted to follow a musical career, but the drawing-board proved to be more magnetic than the bandstand, and he has never regretted abandoning the sax. The nocturnal work habits of the professional musician are still with him, however – he seldom takes up his pen until after dinner and often labours far into the small hours of the morning. By day, he can usually be seen tooling around town in his Porsche. 'I'm kind of a car nut', he confesses.

His favourite serious artist is Paul Klee, whose work he idolizes. Among his fellow cartoonists, he most admires Ronald Searle, Andre Francois, Saul Steinberg and 'some of the younger Europeans'. He is an advocate of the captionless cartoon, which, in his opinion, makes the greatest demands upon both cartoonist and reader and therefore offers the richest rewards. 'I like to let the reader figure it out for himself,' he says. 'I don't like to hold his hand.'

A specialist in the macabre, he naturally feels a kinship with Gahan Wilson and Charles Addams, 'but I think we're all indirectly descended from Goya, Daumier and Bosch'. Many of his cartoons deal with suicide, but Shoemaker does not feel this is a morbid or gruesome preoccupation. 'After all,' he says, 'God tells us, in the Bible, "I have set before you life and death; therefore choose life." By laughing at suicide, I've chosen life – don't you agree?'

We do, and we think you will, too, as you dip into this book of Howard Shoemaker's best work.

The editors of PLAYBOY

SHOEMAKER

OCT
31
HALLOWEEN

SHOEMAKER

"Oh, good grief . . . and I thought he passed the secret formula on to you!"

435
SHOEMAKER

SCHOOL
FOR THE
DEAF
SHOEMAKER
AID
THE
BLIND

". . . I realize this is hardly the time to mention it, but . . . one <u>never</u> wears stripes and checks together . . . !"

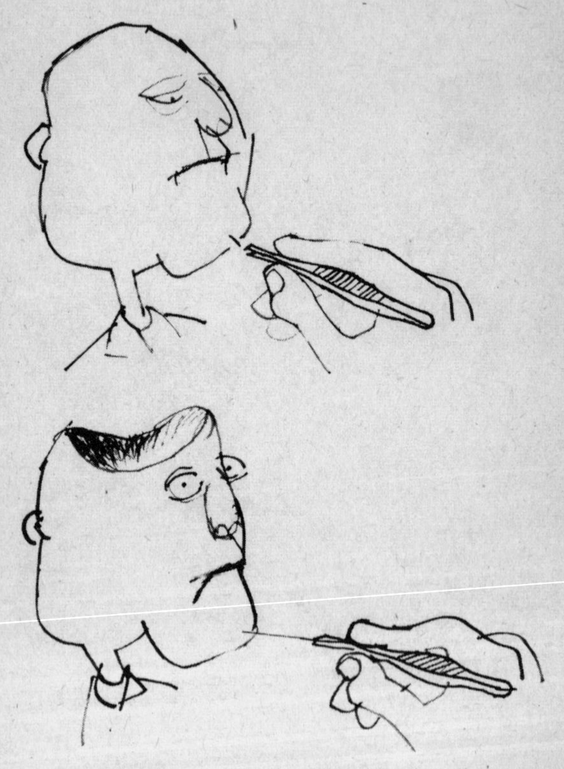

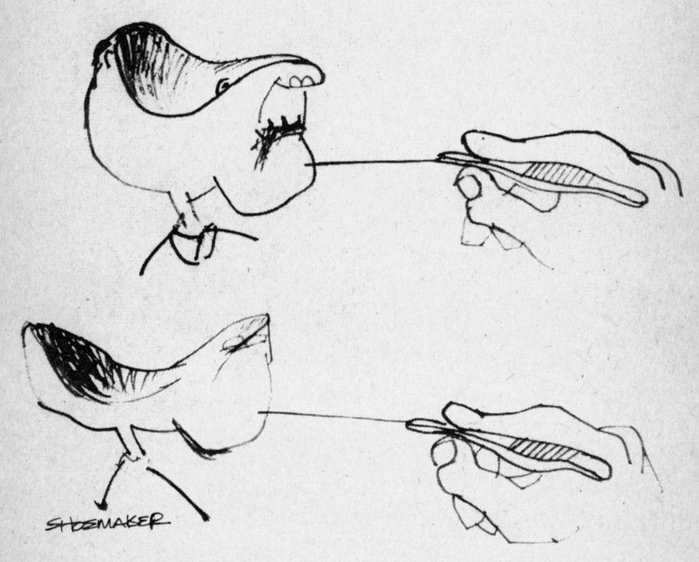
SHOEMAKER

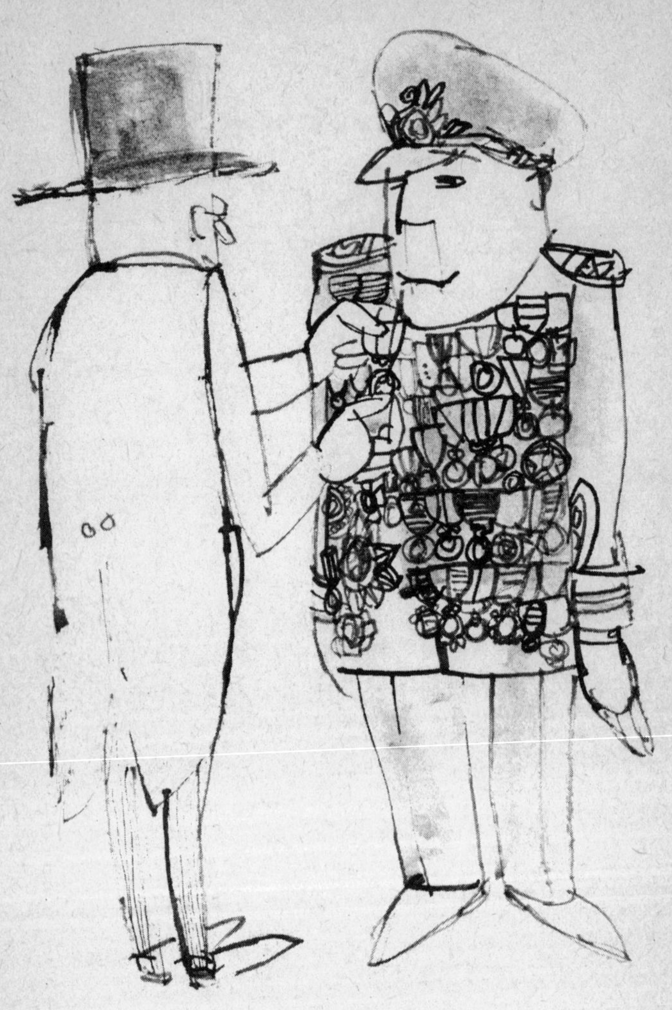

SHOEMAKER

SHOEMAKER

3
4
SHOEMAKER

"No, no . . . she was supposed to get in after you baked the cake!"

'. . . Hello, Audubon Society . . . ?!"

SHOEMAKER

SHOEMAKER

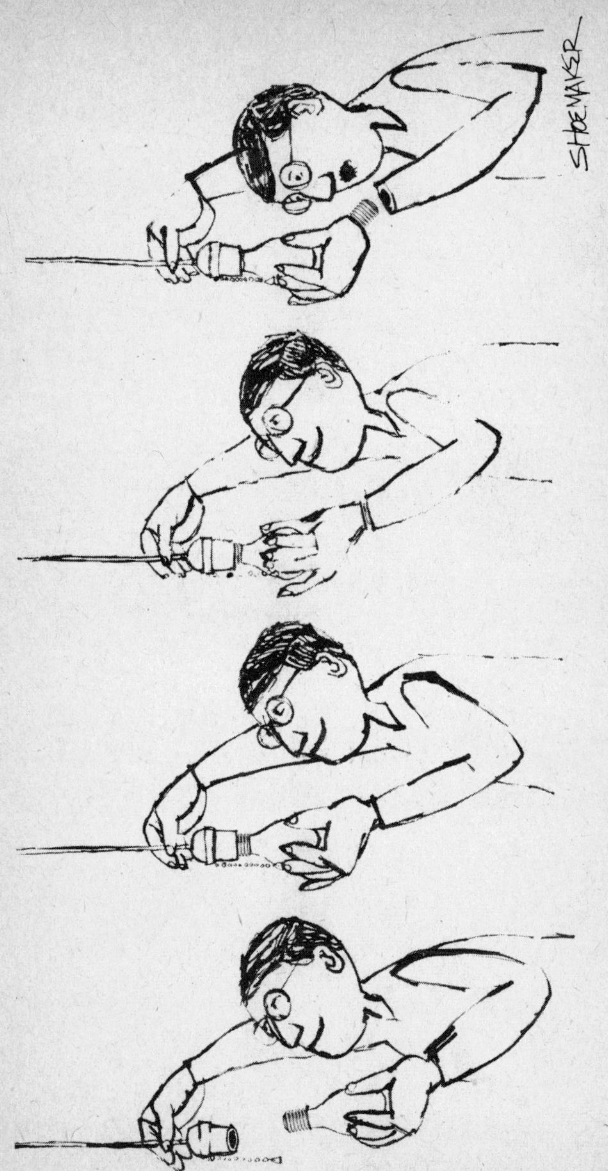
SHOEMAKER

R R
SHOEMAKER

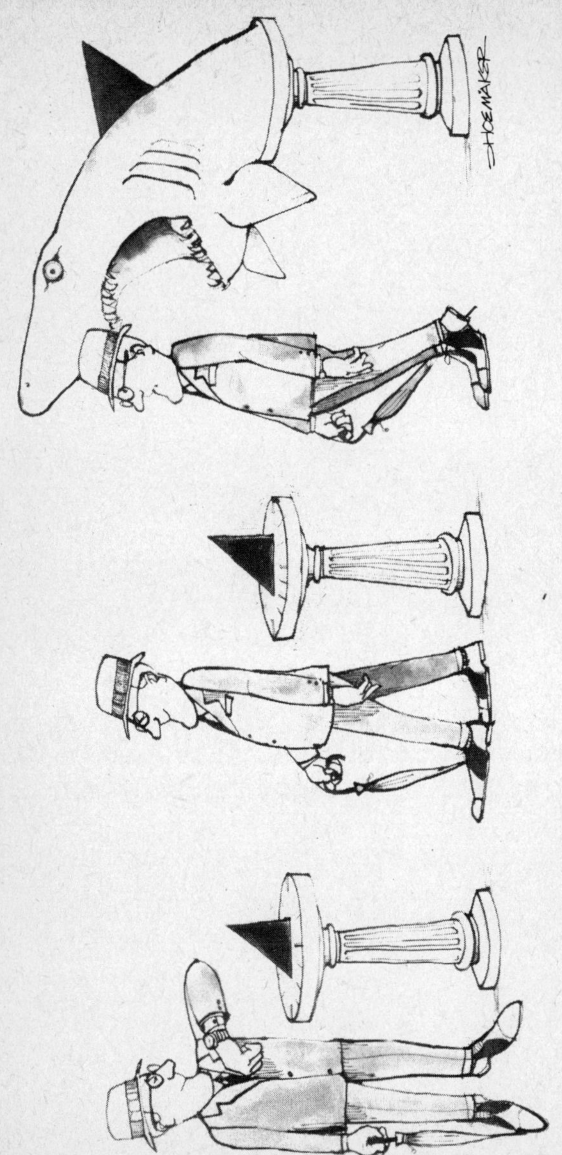
SHOEMAKER

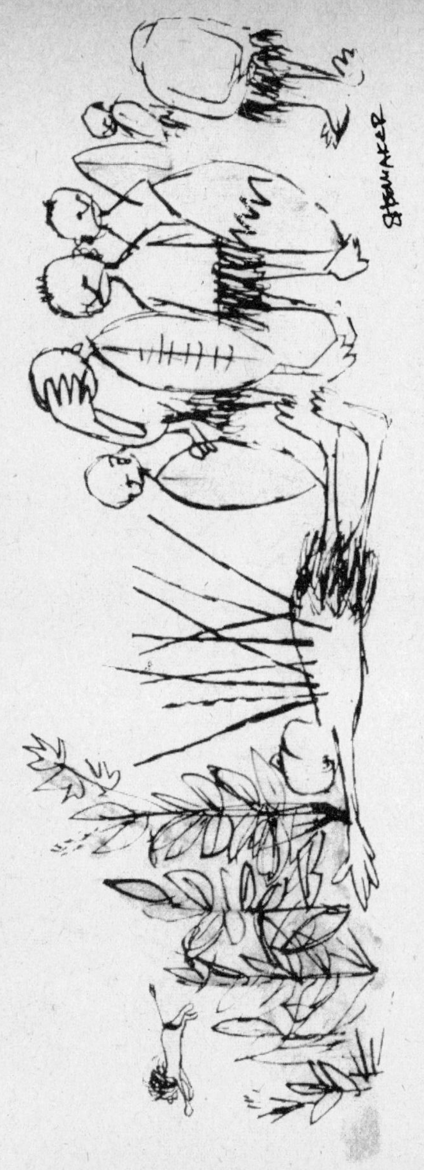
SHOEMAKER

HEAVENLY REST
MORTUARY
HANDY-BAGS
HANDY-BAGS
HANDY-BAGS
HANDY-BAGS
SEAL IN FRESHNESS
SHOEMAKER '68

SHOEMAKER

SHOEMAKER

SHOEMAKER

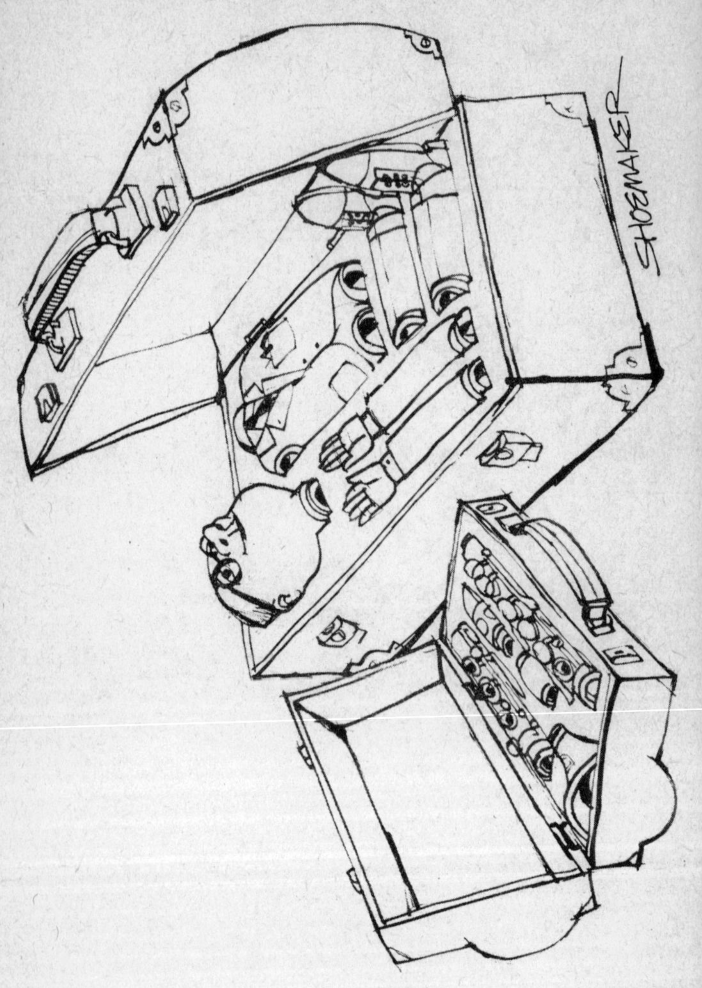
SHOEMAKER

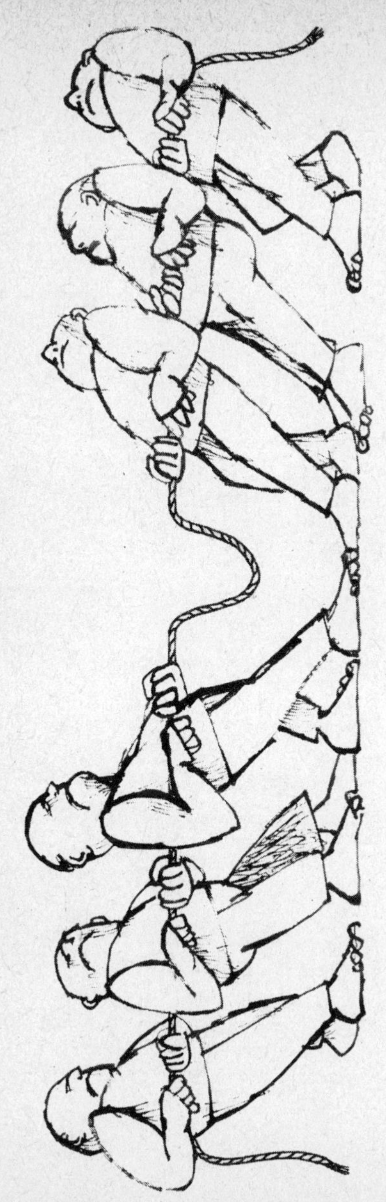
SHOEMAKER

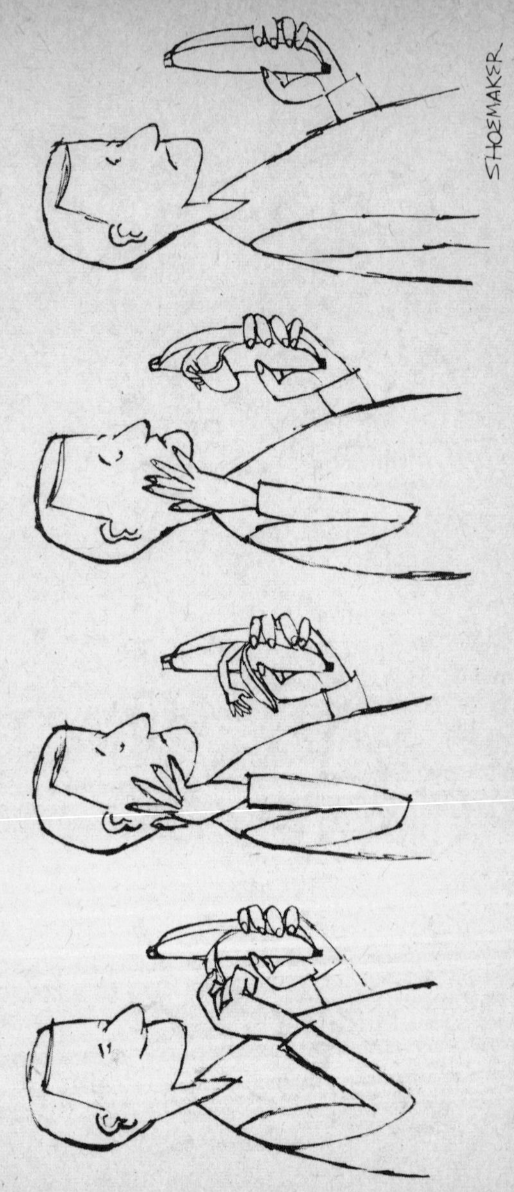
SHOEMAKER

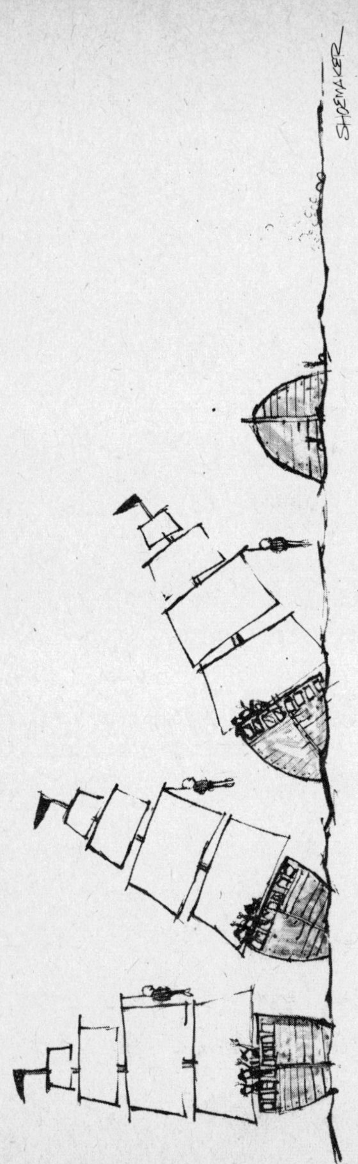
SHOEMAKER

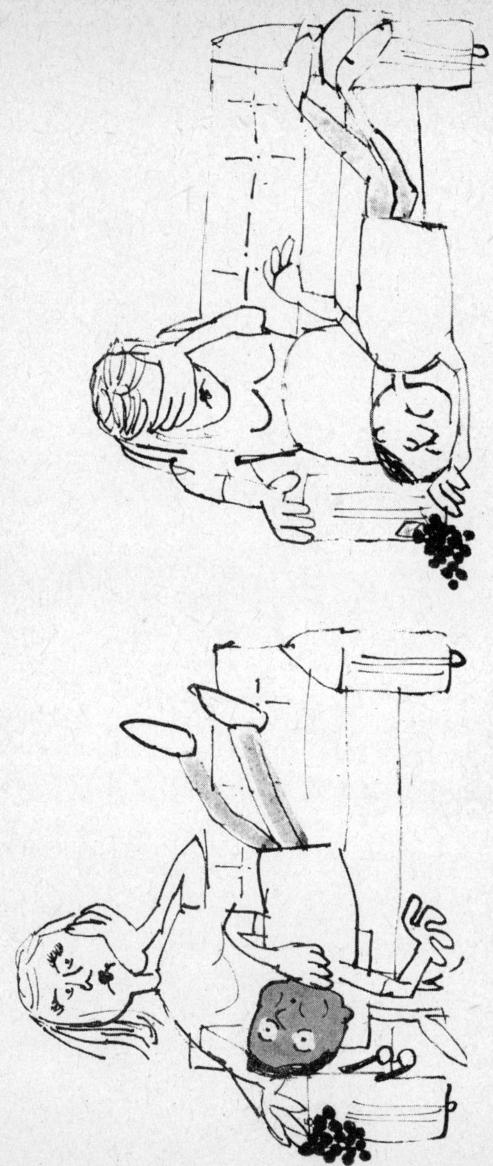

THE SHOELACE

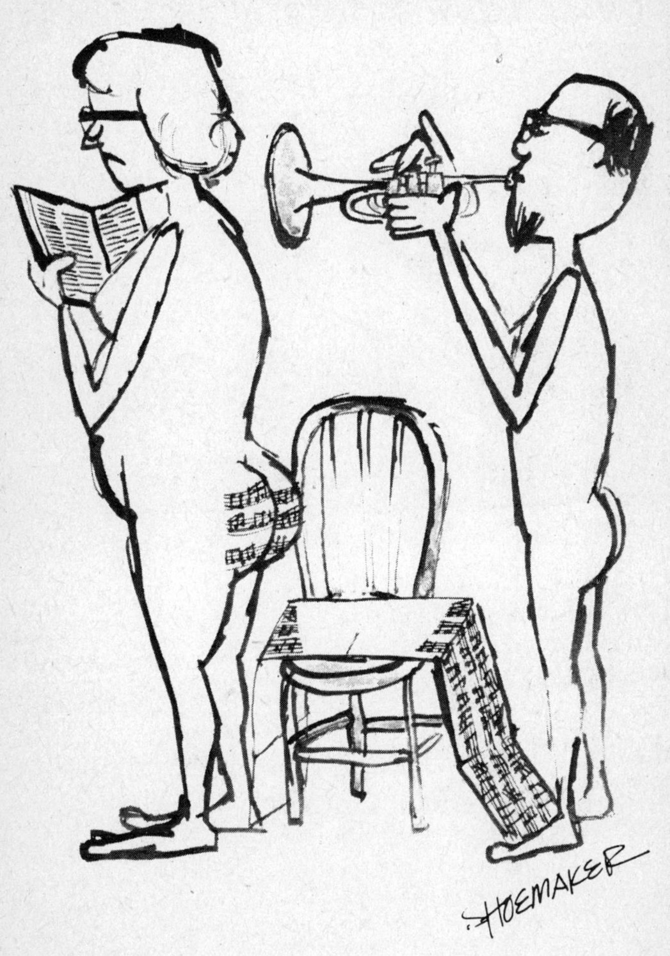
SHOEMAKER

SHOEMAKER

The SWORD IS
MIGHTIE
SHOEMAKER

SHOEMAKER

SHOEMAKER

SHOEMAKER

ZOLE
BROS.
CIRCUS

ZOLE
BROS.
CIRCUS

SHOEMAKER

SHOEMAKER

SHOEMAKER

SHOEMAKER

"Bad news, my King. . . . The Parade of Virgins must be canceled. One is ill . . . and the other refuses to march alone!"

"There's someone here who says he was in the war with you. . . ."

SHOEMAKER

LIVING
BRA
LIVING
BRA
LIVING
BRA
LIVING
BRA
SHOEMAKER

"Happiness is a warm puppy. . . ."

SHOEMAKER

"What are you, some kind of nut?"

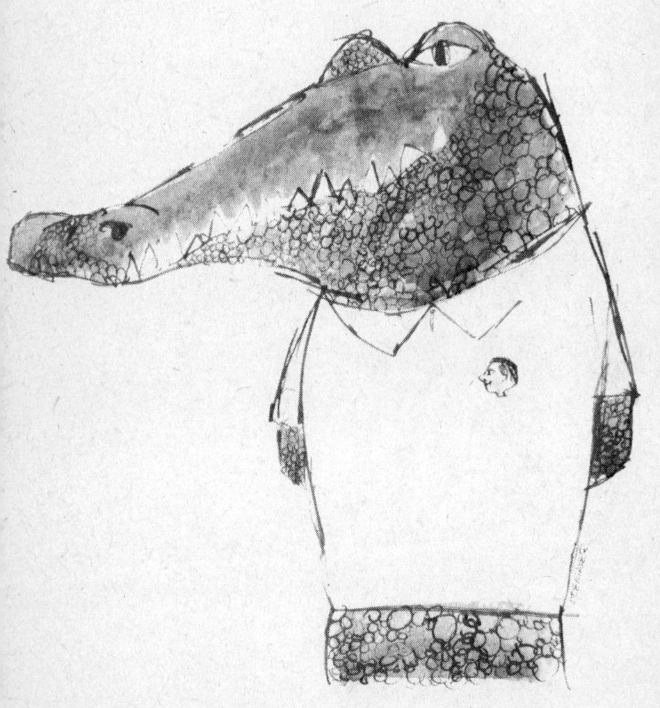

SHOEMAKER

SHOEMAKER

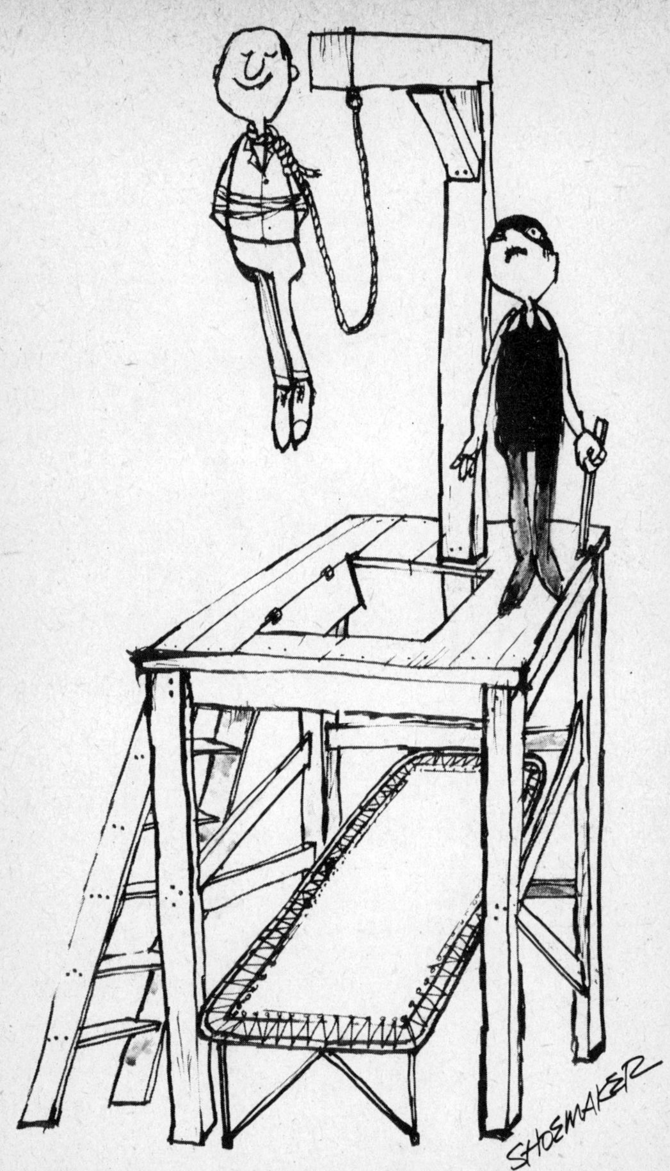
SHOEMAKER

"You knocked?"

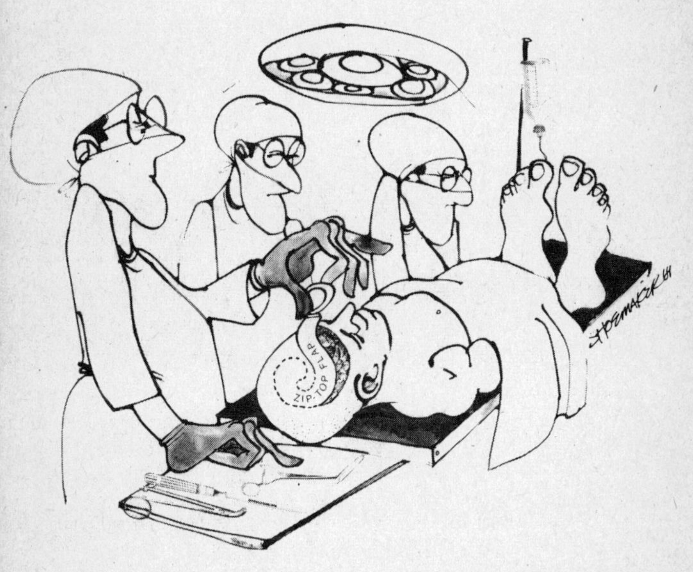
ZIP-TOP FLAP

CHASTITY BELTS
$285 AND UP
SHOEMAKER-

SHOEMAKER

SHOEMAKER

CUSTOMER
ENTRANCE
SHOEMAKER

CRACKER
INTRA-
UTERINE
DEVICE
SHOEMAKER '69

SHOEMAKER

SHOEMAKER

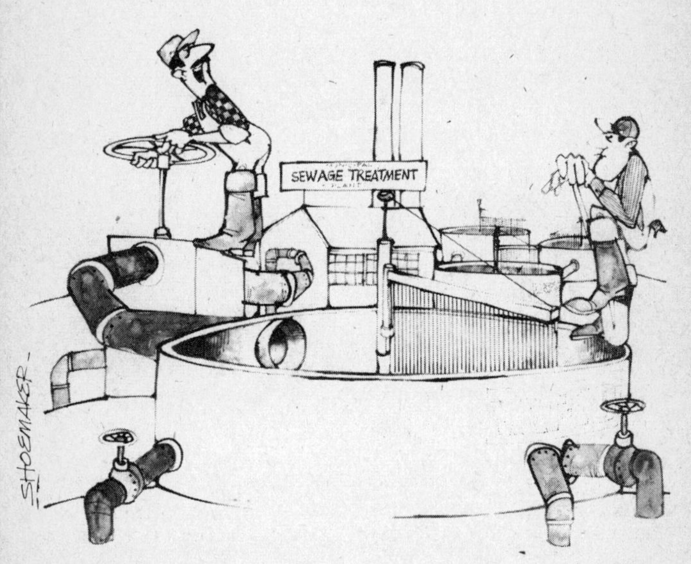

"Here come de sludge!"

DANGER
PIRANHA
SHOEMAKER

"I can't stand his holier-than-thou attitude."

Raymond Erbly
Born Died
12-4-1908 8-21-1961
Beloved
Husband
SHOEMAKER

DROP
THE
BOMB

THIS AD
SPONSORED BY
ACME SHELTERS
TOP-TIP WHOLESALE
FOODS
AJAX
EXCAVATING
CO.
SHOEMAKER

"And what seems to be bothering you?"

"Well, Doctor, you see, I have this man under my feet. . . ."

JUST
MARRIED
SHOEMAKER

GARBAGE
DISPOSAL
ON
SHOEMAKER

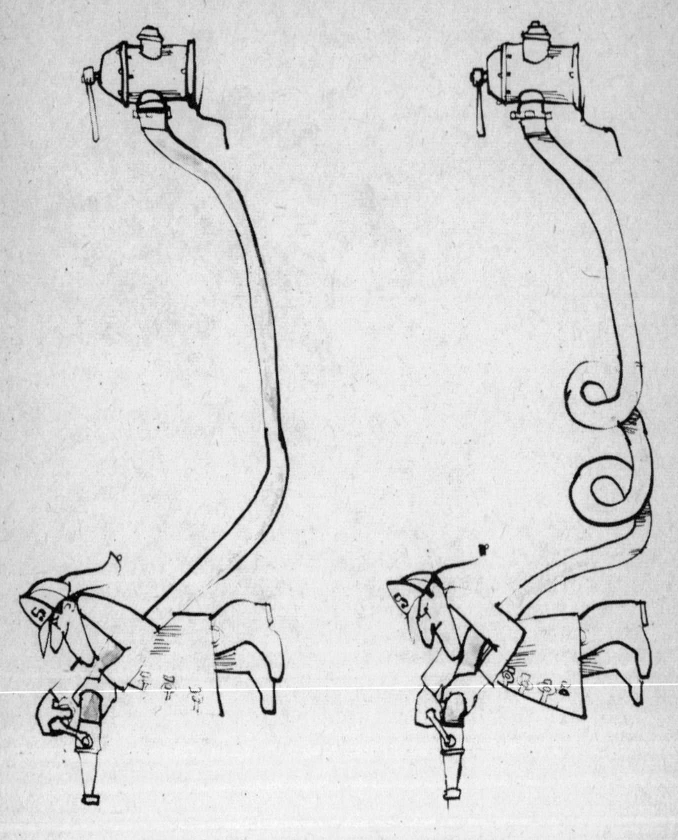

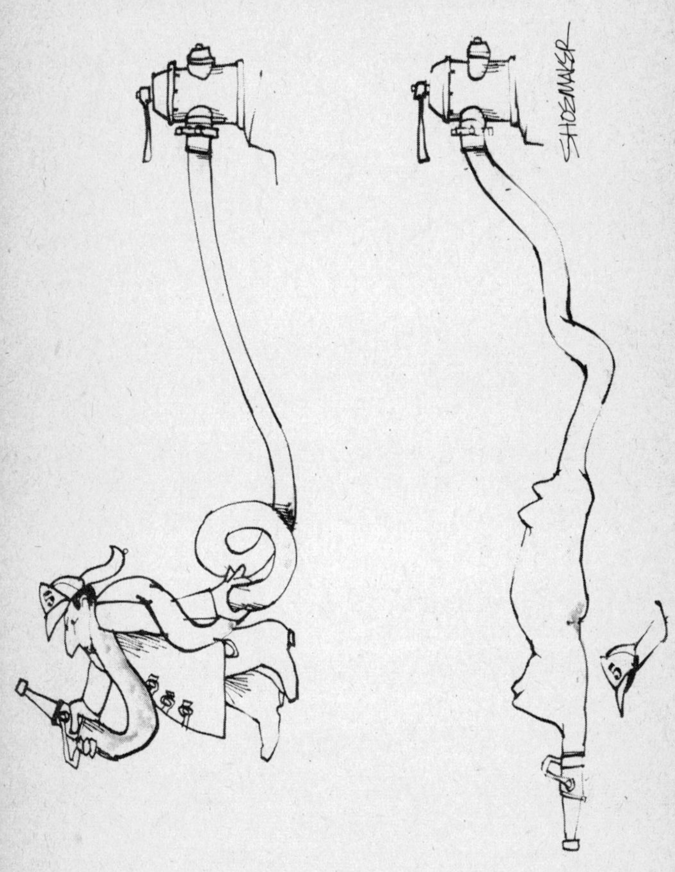
SHOEMAKER

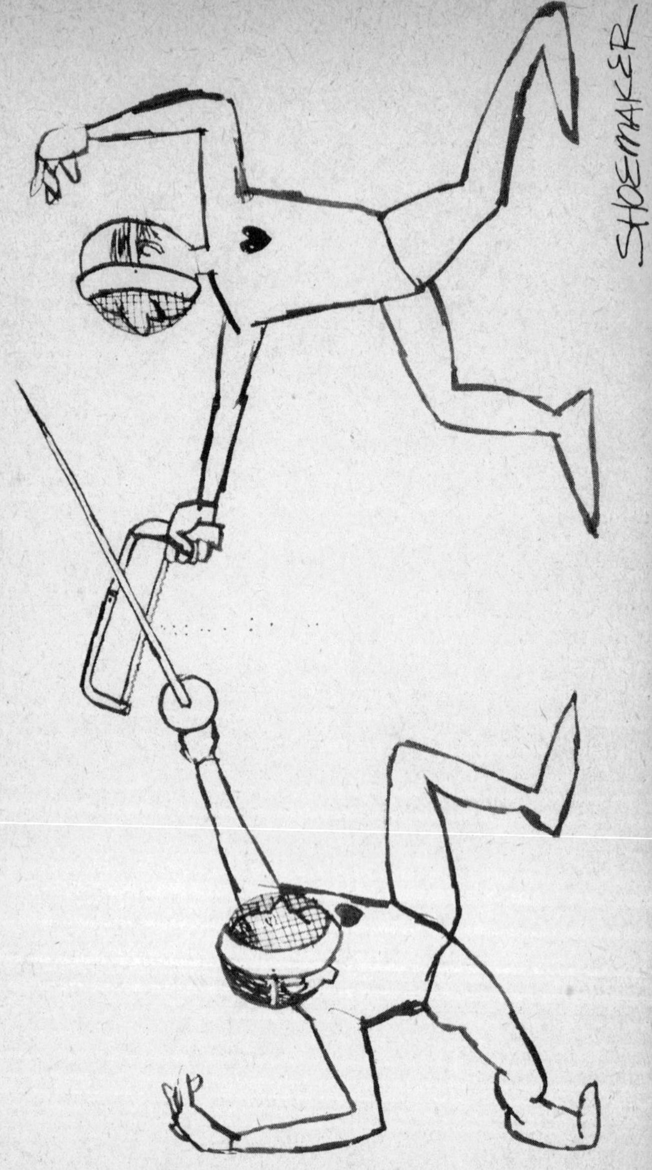
SHOEMAKER

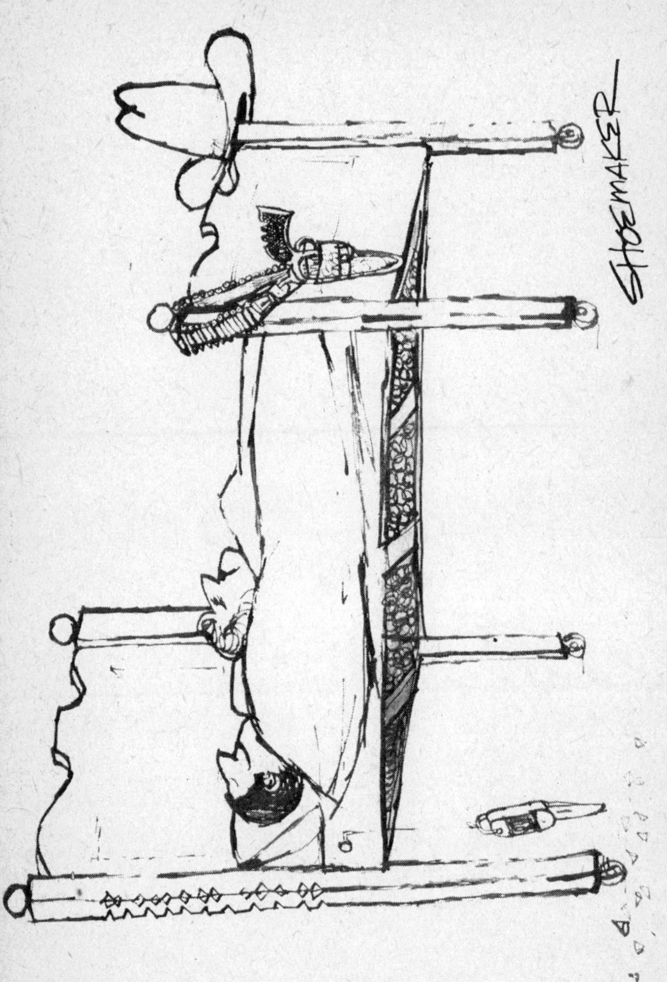
SHOEMAKER

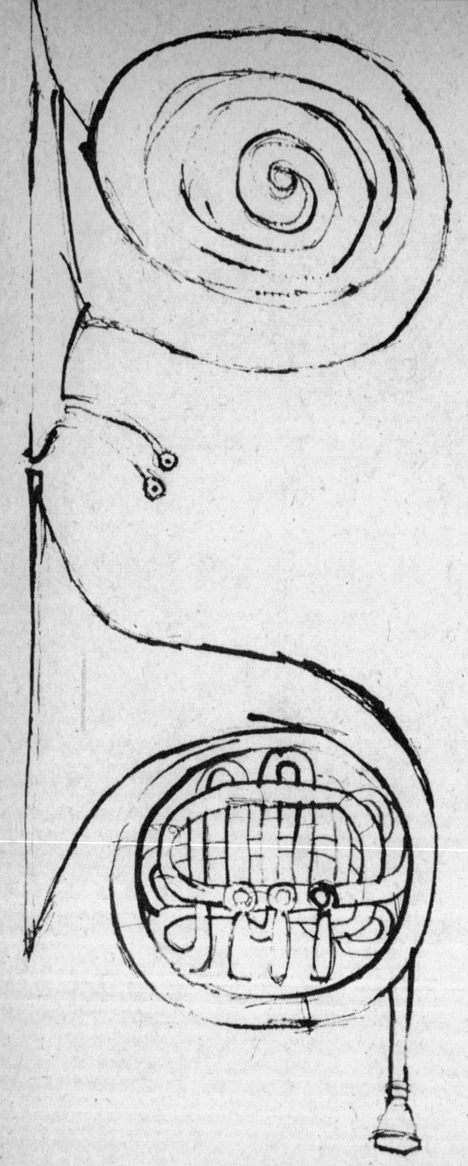
SHOEMAKER

"Will the real condemned murderer please sit down. . . ."

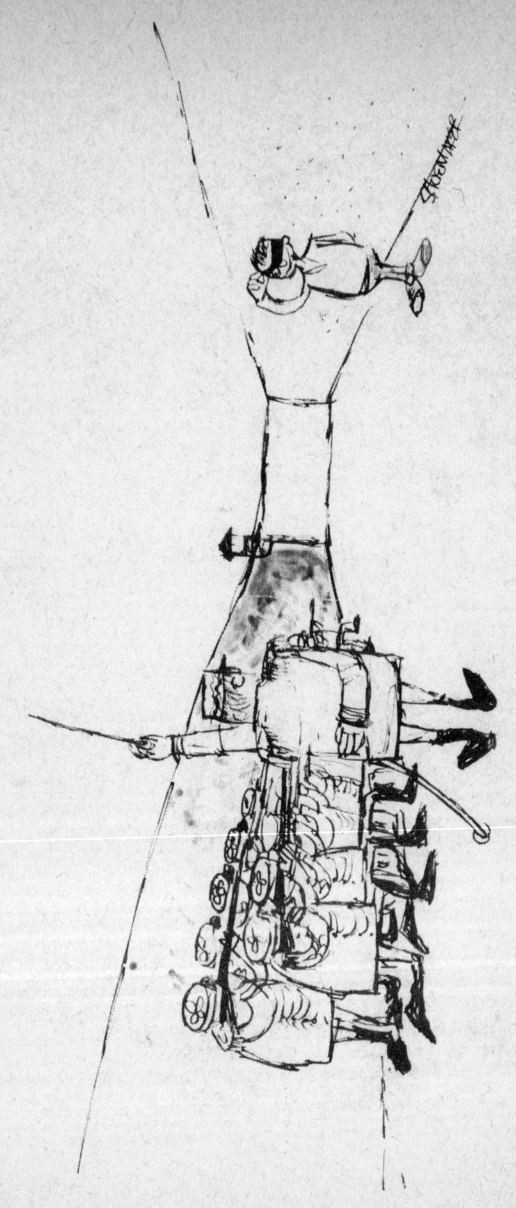

Tom
Chuck
HONEST
WEIGHT
RIB ROAST
T-BONE STEAK
NEW-YORK CUT
BRISKET
CHUCK ROAST
SIRLOIN
PORTER-HOUSE
RUMP ROAST
ROUND
GROUND BEEF
FLANK
SHOEMAKER

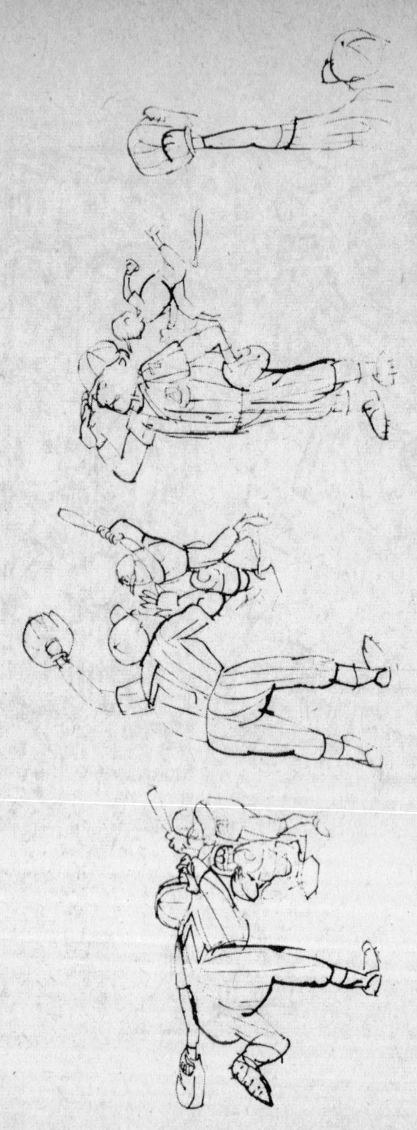

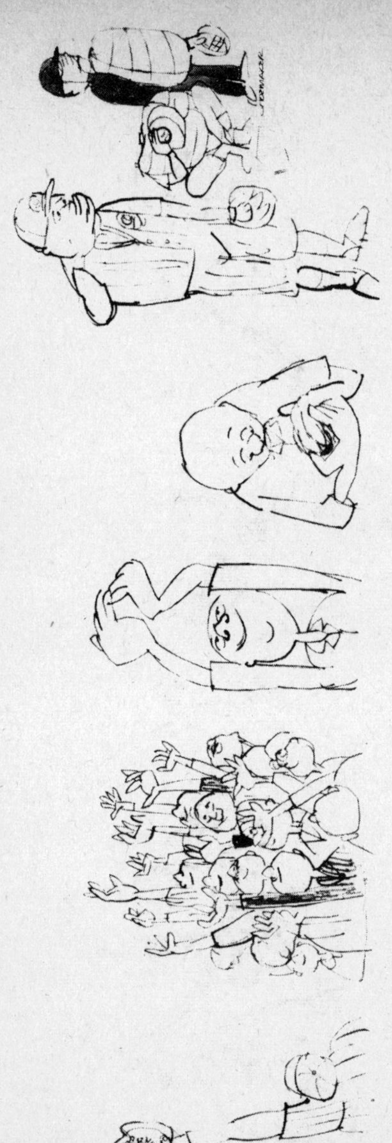

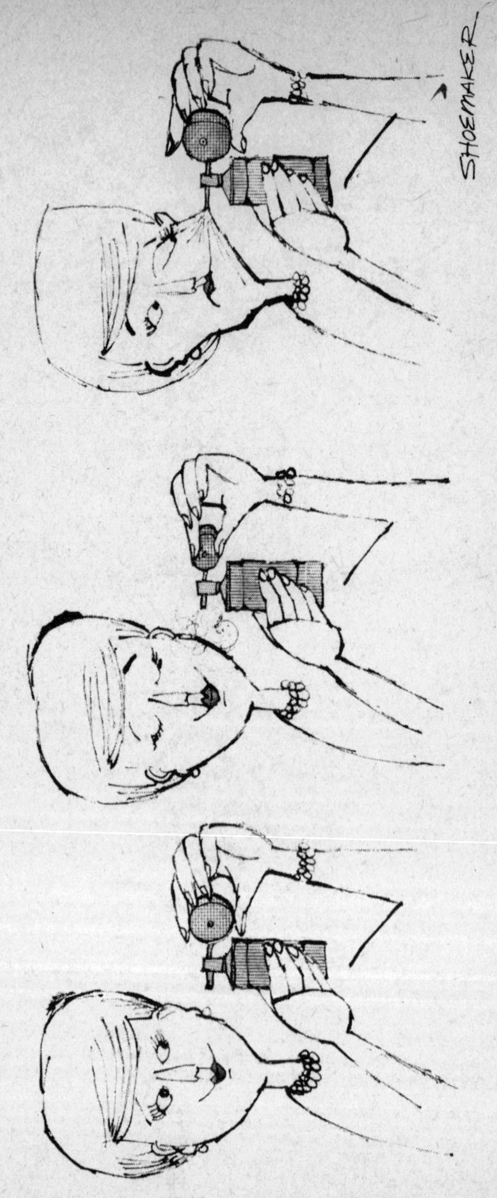
SHOEMAKER

SHOEMAKER

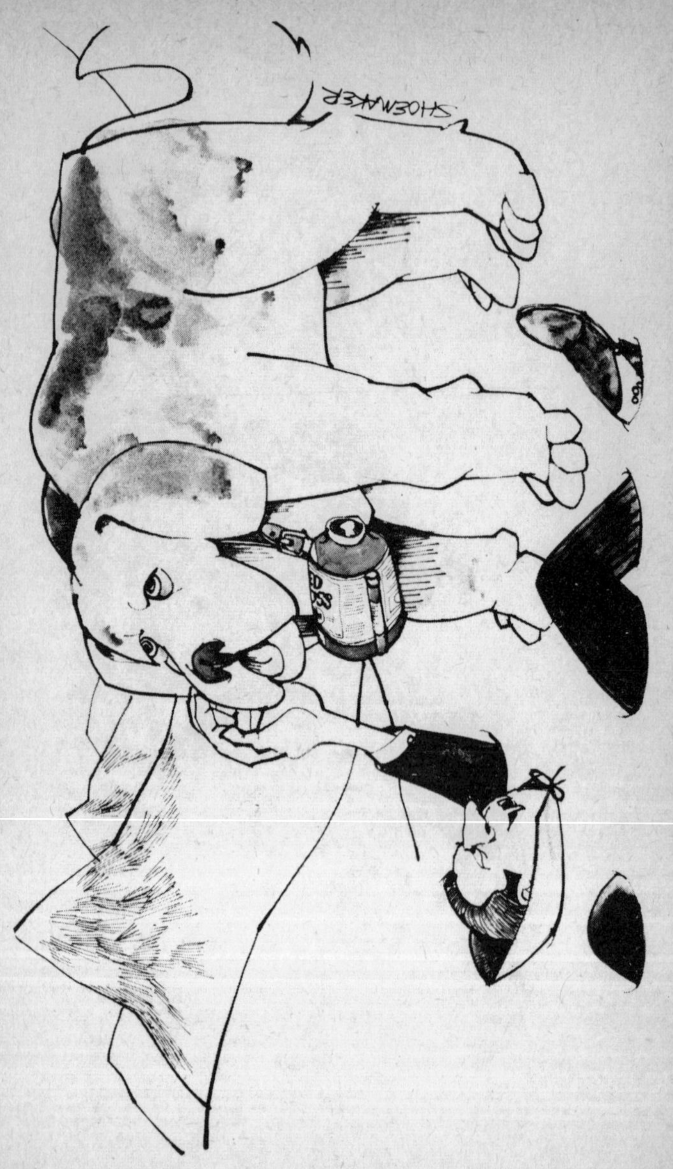
SHOEMAKER

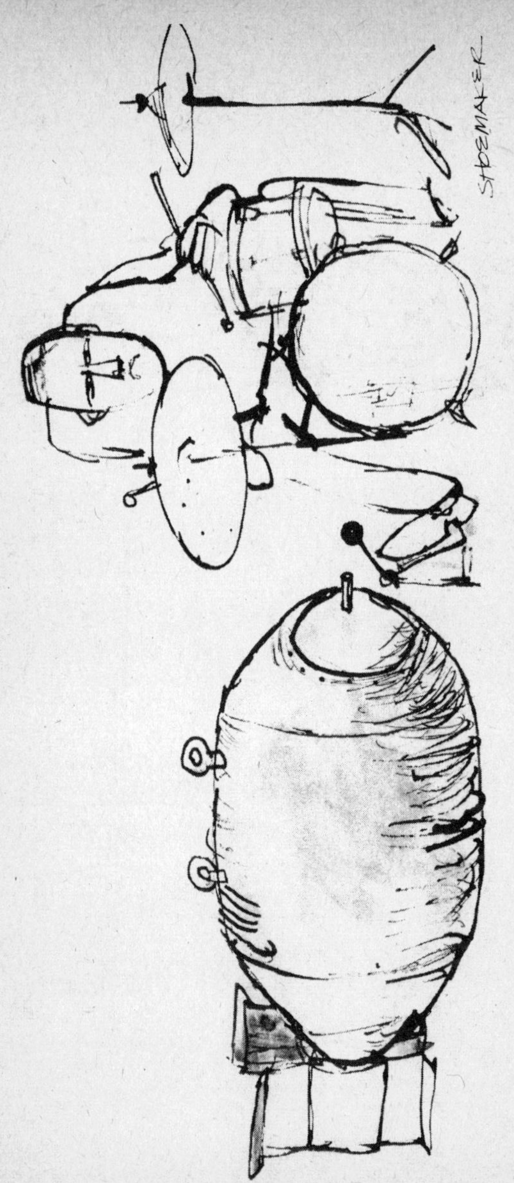
SHOEMAKER

SHOEMAKER

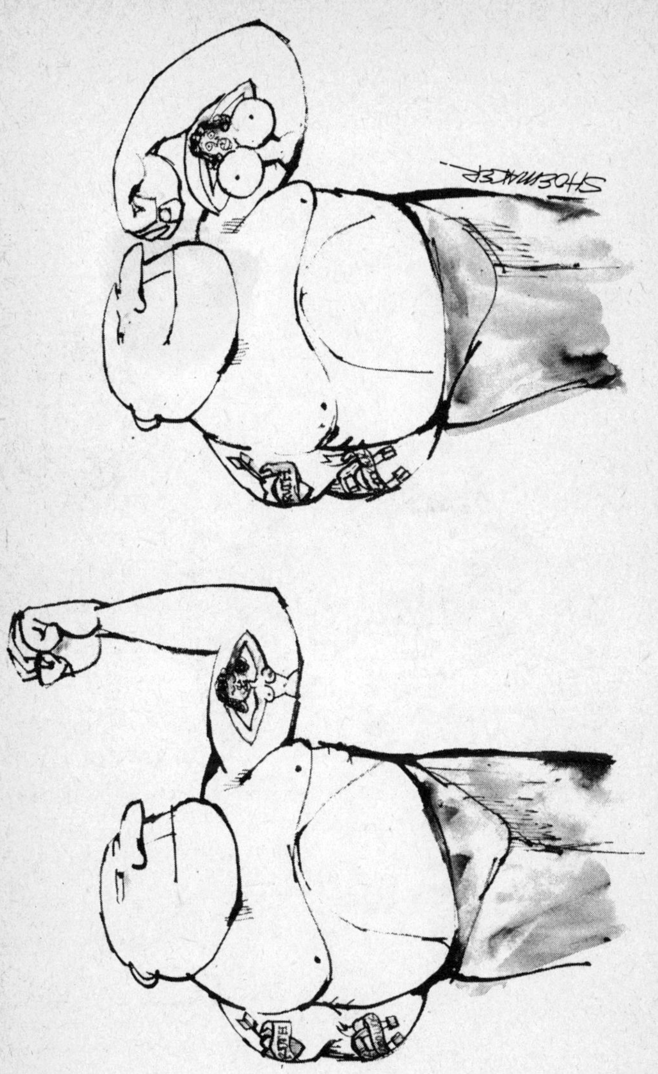
SHOEMAKER

STOP
19 735-1 31
SHOEMAKER

SHOEMAKER

SHOEMAKER

SHOEMAKER

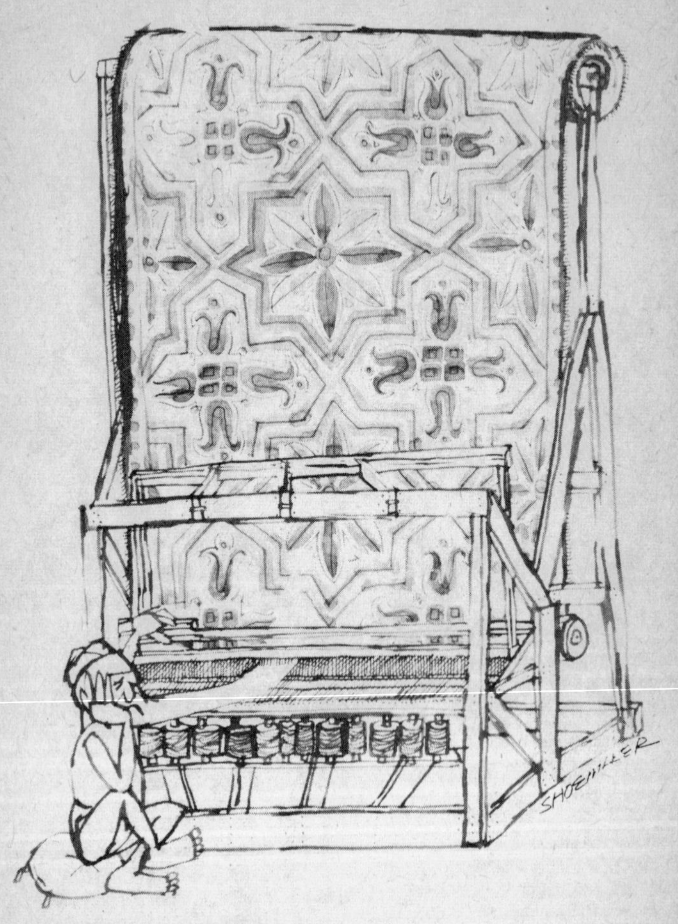
SHOEMILLER

ONE PERFORMANCE ONLY
THE GREAT GONZALES
15¢

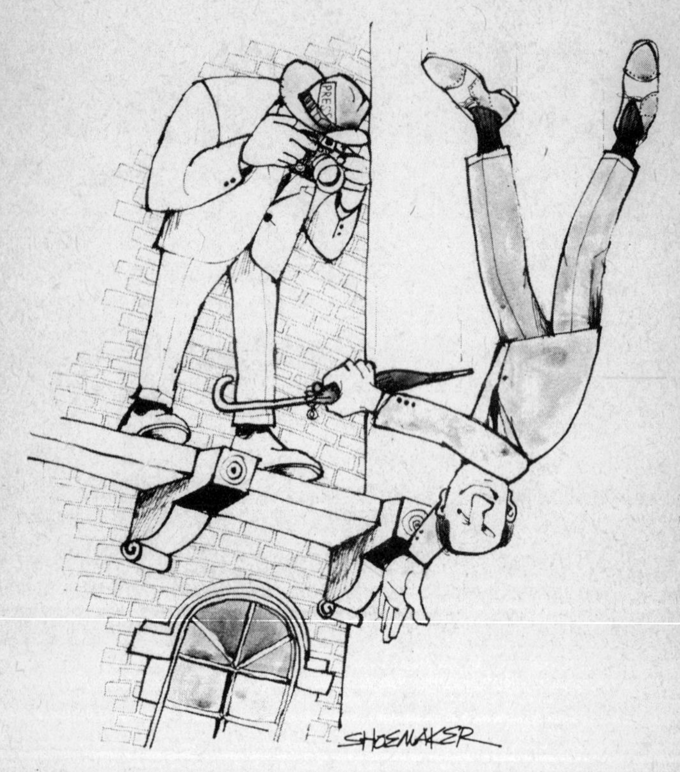
SHOEMAKER

SHOEMAKER

"23, 24, 25 . . . and a pinch to grow an inch!"

SHOEMAKER

SHOEMAKER

SHOEMAKER

ACME
CASKET
COMPANY
EST. 1907

SHOEMAKER

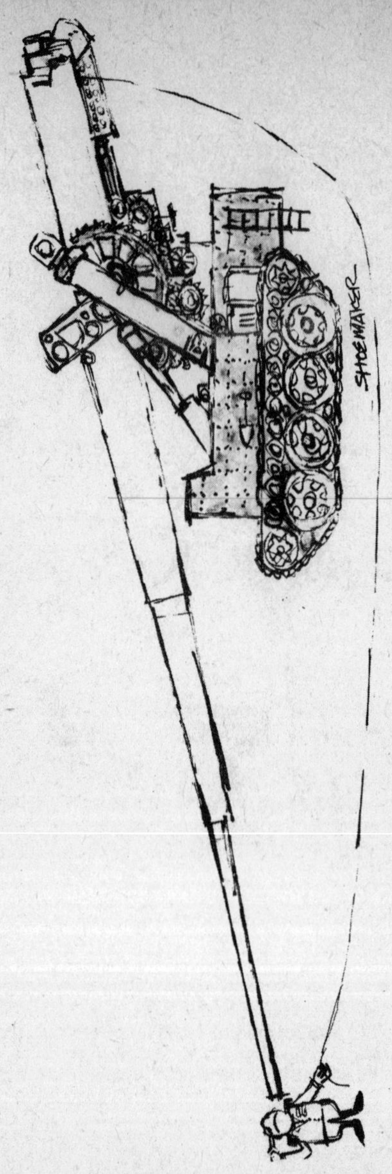
SHOEMAKER

SHOEMAKER

SHOEMAKER

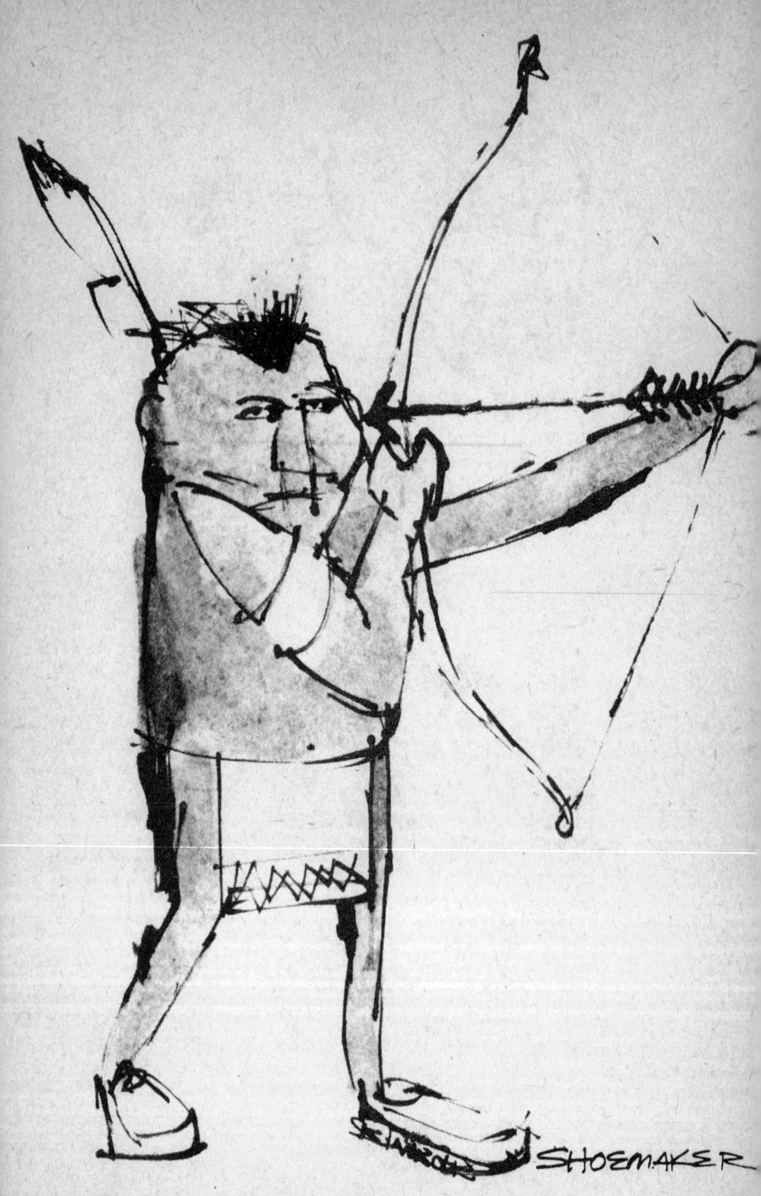
SHOEMAKER

SHOEMAKER